praise for *A Woman Talks to Her Tongue* …

This book—packed with ardour, passion and unflinching honesty—explores and mourns trauma and betrayal, the shock of revealed family secrets. These are poems that allow oppressed voices to be heard, those trapped in cultural or domestic situations that steal agency and dignity; they are inflected with a wide range of intelligent remembering and insistent compassion. The imagery is exacting, sparkling, sifted through an inventive mind, a searching heart. It is impossible not to deeply admire this collection and to welcome its elegance and power. A remarkable debut.

—JUDITH BEVERIDGE

These shimmering poems pluck the extraordinary from the ordinary; they explore the power of silently smouldering family secrets. Gorman shows us how pain so often sits just beneath the veneer of beauty, then surprises us with a form of beauty in exposed pain. In a book about language and a lack of it, these poems use voice as a form of repair, and articulate how we live—no, not just live but are truly alive—while resolutely holding on to the darkest part of our histories. These poems will stay with you for good.

—MARJORIE LOFTI

The tongue, trapped by lies and silence, heavy with unspoken trauma, is released by poetry to "say only / what is true." Here, family histories are spoken and truth-tellers from other times and places gather to tell of bullies and secrets. This chorus of triumphant and mournful defiance is counterpointed by melody, by lyrical flashes of sensuality and ecstasy. A celebration of hard-won and cherished love collects at the heart of this wise and generous debut.

—FELICITY PLUNKETT

A Woman Talks to Her Tongue

A Woman Talks to Her Tongue

POEMS

Alison Gorman

First published in 2025 by 5islands Press

For Oystercatcher Enterprises Ltd
8 Belwarra Ave Figtree NSW 2525
5islandspress.com

Cover, Edgar Degas, *Young Woman with Ibis*,
The Metropolitan Museum of Art, New York.
Author photograph, Sally Flegg
Design and Typography, Gerhard Bachfischer

ISBN 978-1-923248-11-3

Printed and bound in Australia
by McPherson's Printing Group

ACKNOWLEDGMENTS

I respectfully acknowledge that these poems were written on Wallumedegal, Garigal and Worimi lands, and I pay my respects to the elders past, present and emerging.

Gratitude is due to the editors of the following publications in which some of these poems, or versions of them, first appeared: *A Patch of Sun: Café Poets Anthology*, *Cordite Poetry Review*, *Grieve Anthology*, *Honest Ulsterman*, *Island*, *Live Encounters: Poetry and Writing*, *Meanjin*, *Mslexia*, *Popshot Quarterly*, *Southerly* and *Southword*.

Thanks to the judges of the following competitions in which these poems were honoured. "*Eulogy on the Flapper*" received the Dorothy Porter Prize, 2016. "*A Woman Talks to Her Tongue*" was a finalist in the Mslexia Poetry Competition, 2022. "*Onion*" was shortlisted in the ACU prize for poetry, 2022. "*Bully*" and "*Glamour Nails*" were shortlisted in the Bridport Flash Fiction Prize, 2023. "*The Urn*" was shortlisted in the Fish Poetry Prize, 2023, and the Bridport Flash Fiction Prize, 2023. "*After 39 Years, a Photograph Speaks*" was shortlisted in the Gwen Harwood Poetry Prize, 2023. "*A Portrait of My Mother as a Butterfly*" was shortlisted in the Bridport Poetry Prize, 2023. "*Origin*" was shortlisted in the Bridport Poetry Prize, 2024.

I am indebted to Mark Tredinnick and Steve Meyrick for publishing my debut collection. Thankyou Mark for your fine editing and support in shaping this manuscript to its best form. Thankyou Steve for your thoughtful, professional communication that let me know my book was in good hands.

My sincere gratitude to Judy Beveridge who opened the door for me to poetry. Thank you for your generosity and friendship, and for mentoring the Monday Workshop group. I am so thankful to this group, who have worked on these poems with me with wisdom and grace over many years.

Thanks, too, to the Small Back Room Poets, who have helped shape many of these poems with extraordinary attention to detail and kindness. To Audrey Molloy, I am forever grateful to you for seeing this book before I could, for your crystalline reading and feedback, and hours of enjoyable conversation and friendship in poetry.

I am grateful to Varuna, The National Writer's House, for a Residential Fellowship that gave me the space and encouragement to work on this collection. Thank you to Felicity Plunkett and Vanessa Kirkpatrick for your inspiring teaching during the Varuna Poetry Masterclasses and to my fellow masterclass poets for your helpful feedback.

Tabadh Leibh to my Scottish poetry family who worked with me on this manuscript during my visit to Moniack Mhor. Special thanks to Marjorie Lotfi, John Glenday and Cáit O' Neill Mc Cullagh for your warm welcome and insightful reading of my work.

Thanks to the young writers I have taught for inspiring me with your shining imaginations and for asking me each week if I had written a book yet.

Finally, deep love and gratitude to my family. To my sister Susie, thank you for being a silver lining in my life. To my husband Charlie and my sons Samuel and Will, thank you your generosity in sharing me with my pen. Thank you for the love and light you bring. In fact, thank you for everything.

CONTENTS

Telling Will 3

I. ABOUT SECRETS

Ghosts 7
Handbrake 8
Carnage 9
Dinner Party, 1973 10
Love Me Do 11
Sister Villanelle 12
Forged 13
Fractured 14
English Scenic 15
About Secrets 16

II. A WOMAN TALKS TO HER TONGUE

A Woman Talks to Her Tongue 19
Eulogy on the Flapper 23
Viva La Vida 25
Ghost Ranch, 1949 27
The Princess of Silence 29
Prosthesis 31
Venus and Mars 32
The House of Vesta 33
Partenza—Leaving 33
Captio—Capture 34
Capillata—Lotus Tree 35
Aurora—Dawn 36
Sacrum Aquae—Sacred Waters 37
Vivum Sepultus—Buried Alive 38

III. AFTER 39 YEARS, A PHOTOGRAPH SPEAKS

Passport 41
Storm Boy 42
Bully 43
Cherry 44
Onion 45
Guan Yu 46
The Last Conversation 47
Everything Has Been Said 48
The Urn 49
After 39 Years, a Photograph Speaks 50

IV. ULYSSES

Coming Home 55
Postcard 56
Ocean Pool 57
Cowlick 58
January Water Dragons 59
Tonight, the Lion is Here 60
Ulysses Butterfly 62
A Life of Birds 64
Sisterhood 65
Rembulan Spa 66
Glamour Nails 67
Quiet Zone 68
A Portrait of My Mother as a Butterfly 69
Barrenjoey 71
Origin 72

BIOGRAPHY 73

NOTES 75

In memory of my mother Louise

We dance round in a ring and suppose,
but the secret sits in the middle and knows.

——ROBERT FROST, "The Secret Sits"

Telling Will

A galaxy of paper moons floats above us,
lanterns casting soft light on our entrees.
I'm guiding a pea flower dumpling

on chopsticks into my mouth, biting the carved
purple pastry to the burst of peanut
and black vinegar, when you ask me.

Telling you about my father is not on the menu.
A mother–son night—eating Pad See Ew,
drinking Singha at Chon Thai.

We're talking about your work at The Pier,
how you love to pull the perfect brew,
the money you're saving.

I'm thinking about how you have matured.
You don't have to tell me. Your words arrive
from another place. Rehearsed,

careful, feeling their way through the dark.
I've practised this moment too. Telling you.
Absent family always present.

On the next table, a young woman's face is lit
by a sudden blaze of birthday candles
on a coconut pandan cake.

And I tell you about him. You listen, walk around
to my chair, hold me. She covers her mouth
with both hands in surprise.

I. ABOUT SECRETS

Ghosts

At the back of my father's shed was a large leather case stored next to some tea chests. I played there often, on the cool floor, making a dog bed from ribbons of wood shavings. The case had always been there, near my grandfather's saxophone and a set of pianola rolls. Rusted locks snapped up like a jack-in-the-box. Smell of camphor and old paper—that feeling in my stomach, like I had stolen loose change from a drawer. A bundle of letters rested on a deep pile of photographs. Faces swished around my fingers.

Later, my sister told me the tale of two families—each lost a parent. Two widows met, married and made a new family. I can't remember what my father said when I showed him a picture of the man with a moustache leaning against a jet fighter. And when I asked about the pretty woman with soft rolls of hair framing her face, I only recall my mother's lips, frozen in a red line.

Handbrake

I'm six, and you're eleven.
Our mother parks her boxy Corolla
outside the newsagents. The road is flat,
like it's been eyeballed with a spirit level.

She counts coins from her unzipped purse,
pencils the expense in her notebook
and speaks an instruction I can't remember.
Perhaps it's easier to leave her two daughters

in the car needling and elbowing each other
on that vinyl seat, until one of us claims
the space—measured in stitching—we think
we deserve. I watch her swish away

from the car towards the headline bills
and lotto ads, and I long to follow her,
to browse Holly Hobbie swap cards
and smell the strawberry-scented erasers.

Instead, I watch you climb into the front
seat and wait until you catch my gaze
in the mirror. *Don't tell*, you say,
lowering your hand onto the brake,

resting a finger on the button. *I'll let go*.
You feign release and laugh. I close my eyes
and scream, my throat wide open like the foxgloves
that bloom years later in your garden,

the day you tell me what our father did
to you. Our mother returns.
Keys open the car.
One day we'll all crash.

Carnage

just like a volvo
safe and reliable
spacious enough
five daughters
a black tongue
an occasional storm

no one saw it coming
a mack truck
our crumpled carapace
wheels spinning
blown airbags
spangles of windscreen
leaking oil pooled
a flickering flame
threatened

the therapist said
such injuries
critical
it was difficult
for the rest of us
internal wounds
a tangle of scars

we all knew
a man
t-boned

our family
suited to difficult terrain
carried a mother a father
rolling along
road lined with fireweed
cloud overhead

the disclosure that is
on the wrong side of the line
found overturned
radiator hissing like snakes
stuffing the car
on the road
in rainbows
in the busted engine
fire

he'd never seen
one sister fatal
for another
to know the damage
invisible contusions
that would thicken
into purpled flesh

who was driving
pale with shock
by truth

Dinner Party, 1973

My mother bends to place a tray of devils on horseback in the oven. Snug prunes swaddled with bacon and fastened with toothpicks. Heat pours from the open door and ripples the silk of her paisley culottes. She's a kaleidoscope in tangerine and gold. Baby vol-au-vents stand ready, their asparagus resting in bechamel. *Careful, they're hot*, she says, and passes me one on a napkin. I sit on the kitchen bench, swing my legs, and watch her arrange the rest on a wooden tray, tufted with parsley. I bite into buttery casing and shards of pastry litter my pyjamas.

This is where she's been all day—in the kitchen piping boiled Dijon yolks into rubbery white halves and flecking them with caviar. Scooping and chopping the sweet flesh of pineapple to create her rice salad. She's been broiling and braising blanquette de veau, which she'll keep warm through dinner on her electric buffet tray. And there are spatchcocks in baskets, wearing tiny paper slippers. I'm thinking about the dessert hidden deep in the fridge. Chocolate mousse and a biscuit torte. I want to stay up late enough to watch brandy burst into a riffle of blue flame on crepes.

My father is in the good sitting room, preparing the bar in his teak cabinet: stuffed olives, toothpicks and beer nuts. Freshly showered and sharp with Old Spice, his shirt tight and patterned with sunsets, palm trees and a half-naked lady. Singing along a little out of key, he dances an awkward cha-cha, while Sinatra croons a bossa nova from the HiFi. *Tall and tan and young and lovely*. He drops three clinks of ice into a shaker and shakes, pours in vermouth and gin—a splash of this, a splash of that—strains his martini into a glass.

Before the guests arrive my father sinks into his favourite armchair and, with the plop of an olive, his work is done.

Love Me Do

—for Susie

A photograph sits on my desk, its silver-plated frame
collecting dust and spots of tarnish. I keep it in front

of the window, which is bright with garden and a skyline
of shifting trees. If I place the frame on a slant, the morning

sun can't complicate your gaze with light and reflection.
You smile love down the lens, as you hold a baby,

your firm hands pressing the bundle to your hip
like a prize. You're on the front patio, outside

the good sitting room where sometimes you listen
to Love Me Do or Hey Jude on the Panasonic.

Just behind, sits the old stone wall and a silver birch
shimmering in full leaf. It's before school, and you wear

a plaid uniform with a neat jumper. Your hair
is bobbed with a perfect kick of curl that rests against

your cheek. Perhaps you fed me my morning bottle.
I am as plump as a double rose. My round face

and chubby legs spill from a swaddle of nightgown.
Now, I pick up the photograph for a closer look.

I can tell it's our father taking the picture, advising you
how to stand and clicking his fingers to catch my gaze.

We are somewhere else beyond that moment,
my small left arm tucked around your waist.

Sister Villanelle

—for Jinnie

I see you there, between my son's front teeth—
a gap that seems to widen as he grows.
Two tombstones rise from thick pink flesh beneath.

That year we hiked across the alpine heath
and woke to find our hut was deep in snow.
I see you there between my son's front teeth.

You loved a man and Jesus (your sweet relief).
You sang His music brightly. Your whole face glowed.
Two tombstones rise from thick pink flesh beneath.

I watched you draw a needle from its sheath,
inject your thigh. Each day the bruise would show.
I see you there between my son's front teeth.

The day you got the call, I could not breathe—
an organ packed on ice to stem the flow.
Two tombstones rise from thick pink flesh beneath.

And now I watch him smile (my silent grief)
recall you wave and mouth a soft hello.
I see you there between my son's front teeth.
Two tombstones rise from thick pink flesh beneath.

Forged

Our volcano is buried in silence. A quiet that muffled decades
yawns wide. Three sisters have each played a part.

One day we'll meet at our mother's deathbed.
I recall: lock the closet, lock the door, tie the handles

with a dressing-gown sash so we can curl around each other
on the bed, read a book, wind hair with my little finger,

trail it across my top lip: one sister reading in the soft room,
padded with story, the other erupting outside.

One day she kicked the door in, put her foot clean through
the plywood. Our father covered the hole

with a plastic vent, screwed it on firmly. Sudden rupture.
Hot ash and lava escape the magma chamber.

Our estrangement forged in fury. How hard we have set.
Black diamonds, our father lit aflame.

Fractured

My father walks ahead carrying a bouquet of long-stemmed roses.
Clouded eyes look for a number he can't read. He hauls his frail
body down the hospital corridor. In room 19 my mother lies, leg
pinned and plated around a fracture that spirals through her femur
like a corkscrew. Her hospital door is beige and mute. He juggles
his walking stick and the roses, reaches for the handle. Leaning
over the bed, he kisses my mother. I unwrap the roses to strip
away thorns. At the bedside, I hold her bruised hand. It is
cool, and it twitches as she talks a tap- dance through a morphine
haze about the marvels of medicine, the ease of frozen meals, a
grandson who drives too fast. She flings off the sheet, shows the
neat suturing of her swollen yellow thigh. *I'll be home in a week.*
Outside the door, it is quiet. We pass a doctor holding an Xray
up to a box of fluorescent light. His eyes study the damage.

English Scenic

As a child I could hear water
tumbling over rocks, horses
nickering as I forked green peas
into mashed potato.

A green floral farmyard scene
on a plate with a scalloped rim.
Two horses drink from a stream,
a foal resting against its mother.

I never noticed the gabled barn
and farmhouse set among crooked
limbs of oak, the jagged silhouettes
of Scots Pine. Nor the wildflower border

blooming Burnet roses with heart
shaped petals. My father's gift
to my mother. A dinner set
to gentrify our Australian home.

Plates for her to serve seven.
Bowls filled with cinnamon porridge.
Side plates of freshly baked date loaf,
spread thick with whipped butter.

But it is the dinner plate, I think of.
Foil-wrapped apricot chicken on rice.
Ready to reheat for my absent father,
late home from work again.

The plate slammed onto linoleum,
shards of English Scenic scattering
like the loose gravel in our street
as my mother drove away.

About Secrets

I can't tell you anything about the afternoon
I stood at my sister's front door, admiring her garden—

the blue delphiniums and the silvery fuzz
of lamb's ears that crowded the brick path.

I can't tell you how long I waited for her to swing
the door open, her daughter held to her hip

gumming a rusk and wearing the velvet hat
I had given for her birthday. My sister invited me in

but I can't tell you anything about that. We drank tea—
Earl Grey from bone china dressed in rosebuds.

We sat on her floral lounge, sunlight pouring in
through clean windows, the child unsteady

around the coffee table. I can't tell you what we ate.
Perhaps it was her famous apple cake, thick

with cinnamon crumb, or my mother's scones
complete with clotted cream. I can tell you

she placed her cup precisely back in the saucer
and cleared her throat. I noticed more flowerbeds

outside, the riot of orange hollyhocks, the open
mouths of snapdragons. I can't tell you what

she told me about our father, when I knocked
my cup, tipped my tea so it pooled on the carpet

in a large brown stain.

II. A WOMAN TALKS TO HER TONGUE

A Woman Talks to Her Tongue

1.

Sometimes I wonder if the cat has caught you,
          swallowed you like an oily sardine.

Perhaps you got lost in the soft cavern of my left cheek,
          waylaid by an avoidance of truth.

It's possible you were tied to the floor of my mouth,
          bound by a too-tight frenulum,

or swollen to silence by an anaphylaxis of sorts;
          an allergy to secrets (not shellfish).

2.

Once, I worked with others like you, prodding
          small mounds of muscle with a flat wooden stick.

I shone a pen-light into each pink cathedral,
          illuminated the curve and fall of palatal arches—Say ah.

The surfaces glistened; blushing mucosa stippled
          with buds (or papillae, if you want to sound fancy),

sometimes coated in pale grey fur from pooling saliva
          and grief that couldn't be swallowed.

3.

Your kind can writhe and flicker, ripple your belly
with unchecked movement—fasciculations.

How neatly the tongue sat in the mouth,
as I checked for signs of deviation.

Please poke out your tongue. This can be difficult
in front of a mirror in a hospital room,

under bright lights where you have met for the first time.
Now, can you move it quickly, from left to right?

4.

Tongues can atrophy like the heart, waste away
with weakness after a single assault.

Exhausted fish caught on a handline, they distort
vowels and insert glottal stops

when you least expect it. Repeat after me: Puh Tuh Kuh.
It's easier if you start off slow, approach

each consonant gently, as though you were rolling
a sea anemone in your mouth.

5.

Can you touch your nose with your tongue? Like this.
Dexterity is needed for mastication.

Now I have your attention! But it's not your eating
I'm interested in. Do you remember

our first kiss? At the school fair, on a wooden bench,
his pimpled boy-face moving closer.

The shock and thrust of it, a wild eel pushed between
our teeth. So curious, that taste of tobacco.

6.

I met a man who had a quarter of a tongue,
still smoked through a stoma in his neck.

We burped his name and the days of the week, one syllable
at a time. Another woke from his coma

sounding like a German pixie. His vocal cords were taut
with damage, his tongue domed in his mouth.

He warped articulations across geography and fairy tales.
There were other tongues too — and then, there is you.

7.

Women have been tortured like this—their tongues
pinned with a Scold's bridle.

What is your excuse? We are neither witch nor hag.
Ignore the muttering inside our head—

set your tip behind our top teeth where No is formed.
Be ready—I want to roll our eyes back and fall

into an ecstasy of words. I will untie you and say only
what is true. Let's whisper glossolalia.

Eulogy on the Flapper

Nobody has ever measured, not even poets, how much the heart can hold.
—ZELDA FITZGERALD

Sweet heart, where are you?
A dusky moon has risen in my window
and it's so damn lonesome here tonight.
They say you're dead and some days I believe it
until my mind declares it's those ghastly
voices again. Soon, the doctor will electrify
me with his fandangled wires. I'll be balled up
and blank as a page but please,
don't despair, Baboo.

Today, I sat outside and painted
the tulip trees and started penning
a new novel. You'd think it swell,
even though you never could see the artist
in me. Ah, let's not fuss with that old quarrel.
I wish it were midsummer and we were diving
into jade and amethyst from the highest cliffs
at Cap d'Antibes or lying in the long citoneuse
beams of the sun on the plage at Juan-les-Pins.

You could drive us too fast
in your borrowed breezer along the winding,
palm-fringed roads of Côte d'Azur until the sky melts
into pink. I can hear the piano and drums calling jazz
from "Villa America," smell the heliotrope
in the air. I'll dress with audacity and rouge.
Let's dance on the terrace, spiflicate
ourselves with mint juleps and sing
a Goofo duet for the others.

We could not repair after Edouard.
He was just an imagining, a folly
to distract me during Gatsby. Like Isadora
combing her fingers through your hair,
calling you *Centurion*. It was a jealous heart
and moonshine that made me burn
all my clothes in the bath. But tonight,
I *love you anyway—even if there isn't any me*
or any love or even any life.

You must be close now.
Come quickly and take me to Cuba.

Viva La Vida

Soon, I will leave you, Diego.
Death will unpin me from this bed

to float with Noguchi's butterflies
into our blue walled garden. I will rest

upon the pyramid among the pots
and cacti, drink nectar from the orange

dahlia that grows between your idols.
I will watch over Casa Azul, and you,

mi amor. But first, I must finish this painting.
It is the sweet, pink flesh of watermelon.

I love the way it hides beneath dark
green skin. Tell me, what shall I call it?

Let it come to me, in my final brush
strokes and I shall write it on this slice.

I want to paint in the garden today,
with the spider monkeys eating fruit

from my hand. I want Bonito to perform
his best parrot tricks for a pat of butter.

Mother said that you and I were a marriage
between an elephant and a dove. But you

are a toad, Diego — the greatest accident
of my life. Not even my sister was safe

in your slippery hands. Bastardo!
I took lovers as balm, but the truth is

I love you more than my own skin.
Promise me that you will burn my body

when I have gone. Ask the women to dress
me in my white huipil, to braid my hair

with flowers and to put on my rings.
Play music and drink tequila. Ask Chavela

to sing Paloma Negra to me. Set fire
to my bed and watch my body burn.

Until then, I will keep painting
words onto watermelon.

Ghost Ranch, 1949

Sometimes, I imagine I lived then.
        I'd travel to Abiquiú
in the spring by train, chug my way
        through the Jemez mountains,
dotted with spruce and boulders
        until I glimpsed views of the Chama,
carving a blue sweep through tundra, aspens
        and cottonwoods in new leaf.

Perhaps I was drawn by paintings
        of the Pedernal, your private mountain,
given to you by God, you say,
        its flinty caprock flat as a canvas.
How do we meet? It doesn't matter.
        Your hacienda is a symmetry of red
earth walls with a lush garden
        of vegetables and jimson weed.

Would you nourish me with a salad
        of lovage? Or prickle like the cactus
on your porch? I want to sit in the cool,
        white room and watch your mountain
change from mauve to deep red.
        We could draw with charcoal or pastels,
drink tea at your dining table and listen
        to Gershwin or Bach.

Maybe we'd talk about the colours
of music or small flowers,
like hollyhock and larkspur, that no one
really sees until you paint them big.
I wouldn't mention my carnal thoughts
when I look at Black Iris
and I wouldn't ask about Alfred (your love)
or those broken months in Bermuda.

Instead, we'd drive out to the cliffs
of the White Place instead, in your Ford
Model A, then walk the pink clay
of the Badlands (littered with pallid
hoodoos and colourless spires),
fossick in the scree for bleached bones
and horn strewn in the tumbleweed.
As you lean back on the limestone cliff,

I'll watch you sketch a cow skull
that you imagine is floating
in the sky.

The Princess of Silence

—after ENHEDUANNA

Bring your ear to these lips
as you wind my thick braid through a headdress
of gold and carnelian. Listen close now, Ilum.

Today, Father will proclaim
I am High Priestess of Nanna-Suen.
O to be married to a moon god!

Brush my eyelids green
and darken the rims with kohl. Shield me
from the evil eye of all who crave my vocation.

King Sargon the Great—
my father and first ruler of Akkad—will tell
this, to men gathered at the Great Ziggurat,

to gaze at the morning moon.
He, who has conquered all of Mesopotamia,
will ask them to bow before me, a woman—

the first woman, to seize
divine power with her hands. Let them see me *clothed*
in radiance and teach them to fear me,

to hold their venom.
For when I speak, *heaven will shake. Open-mouthed*
I shall roar like Iskur at the earth.

Paint my lips with crushed rubies
and hang this chaplet of golden leaves around my neck.
Men will read every hymn I write on clay.

Hymns to praise the temples—
those heart-soothing houses wrapped in beams of light,
where jewelled lapis herbs fleck the shining beds.

O Ilum, lend me your wisdom!
My scribe will arrive soon carrying a well-sharpened reed.
My heart is a *wild cow.*

How can I capture, with script pressed
into clay, the divine wonder of the moon?
I am a great *winged lion pacing the steppe.*

And yet, a *skin of brickwork* will carry
my written word across the high plains to the river.
Something will be created that no one has created before.

Now I am priestess, princess and poet,
they shall call me En-hed-uan-na. But you may call me
Princess of Silence, Ornament of Heaven.

Prosthesis

One eye is a blown bulb.
Venetian glass stitched into a socket

with spools of spiderweb thread.
A mirror. Her mirror. She admires

the engraved iris, patterned with lines
like bursts of touch-me-not.

Dust on a skirting board, bitten quicks
of her fingers, lips of a cheated lover,

foetal fists of babies she chose not
to bear. Absent eye. There are things

she prefers not to see: Fists of dust.
Thin babies. Bitten lovers. They gather

like blood seeds in a pomegranate.
One blink could slice her open.

Venus and Mars

—SANDRO BOTTICELLI, c. 1485

Awake now. Remember our love
in the shade of a wild myrtle forest.
Your red, silk pallium softens our bed
of bracken and leaf. The air is cool here,
broken by swallow song and the hum
of wasps that swarm and crown
your abundant hair. I study your ecstatic
slumber—a sole crease of brow, an easy
parting of lips, your brave span of chest.
I want the burn of your eyes, the brine
of your skin. Far from bloodshed
and the din of battle, you abandon it all:
your lance, cuirass and beloved blue helmet.
Naked and fearless you surrender to me.
A little death that strands you oblivious
to lewd taunts of drunken satyrs. Fat bellied
with goat leg and horn, they thieve, thrust
and sound a conch but still you do not stir.
This is no time for sleep. Gather your strength.
For I am your bright star and when you wake
        I will ruin you again.

The House of Vesta

Partenza — Leaving

To get to the temple, Father and I were borne in a curtained litter, carried forward to Rome by slaves. I recall little of them except the stink of tunic stained by labour, the rhythm and slap of worn sandal on stone. Through gold curtains, I watched Mother stand quiet outside our villa. She held fast the small hand of my brother Lucius as we drew away. At breakfast, our family feasted on bread, figs and honey. Mother did not speak when Livinia (beloved nurse) braided my hair like a bride. Instead, she lay offerings of grapes and pomegranate upon our hearth, watching curls of smoke for divinations from Fortuna. Father declared I would be chosen for my wit and Mother's beauty. The honour! To tend a celestial fire, the beating heart of Rome. The litter lurched and swayed along roads, raising dust while the slaves toiled onward. As we neared the temple, a bronze dome caught sunlight. Crowds sang with trumpets and horn, while girls and fathers climbed stairs to the atrium. Even then, I held my question. I waited for Father to arrange his toga, pick fig seeds from his teeth.

Captio — Capture

I was not used to sitting on Father's lap. He tsked and scolded as I shifted about, searching for comfort on his knee. We waited on a crowded bench in the temple as dark flame made shadows on the wall. My father held me firm as the Pontifex approached sweeping his ample robes past the other girls, all with their proud fathers, just like me. Have you ever seen a man wear a veil? I thought of Mother and the poem we prepared but this was no time for recitation or tricks. The Pontifex stopped in front of us, muttering. As he leaned in to study my face, he tilted my chin, his hands stinking of wood smoke, his breath soured by wine.

> I *take you thus, Amata, as a Vestal priestess.*

Father slackened his grip as the Pontifex seized me. It would be years before I was touched again.

Capillata — Lotus Tree

I thought I saw birds in the branches, their long tails dangling among fruit. The lotus tree flourished near the atrium, where I had left Father, triumphant and glorying among failed men and daughters. The Pontifex pulled my bound hands towards a knot of women who sat beneath the boughs, chatting and braiding hair. They quietened and rose from stools as we approached, their heads bowed and hands hidden in the woollen drape of their stolas. Marcia was the first to step forward. She untied my reddened wrists and gestured to a wooden lectus beneath the tree. As I lay down and closed my eyes, I felt the women gather, undoing and combing the black lengths of my hair. It was the shick and scrape of a cool blade against my scalp that startled my eyes open. Where was Mother? Birds had flown from the tree.

Aurora—Dawn

Most mornings, I rang a silver bell. Artemis came, carrying oil lamps bright with flame. She hung them on the walls and when I was agreeable, pulled back silk blankets. Through open shutters I could view the garden. Even at that hour, the two pools mirrored columns of cypress and the peristyle, where later I would sit and talk with the others amid the gurgle and spray of fountains. Such relief after a long, hot morning of lessons. The Vestalis Maxima demanded silence to illuminate the art of kindling. In the temple, we watched her weave tinder nests and exact a dry twig to fit a notch. She rubbed the spindle between her palms, until a spark leapt, fanned to life by her whistling breath. The old virgin frightened us with tales of dying flames and grumbled when I whispered with Licinia. We could not wait to run free outside, to chase each other among gardens of rosemary, and startle peahens as they wandered through flowerbeds, feeding on bursts of marigold.

Sacrum Aquae—Sacred Waters

This morning, two of us left the temple to fetch water. Scented flames towered at our backs, billowing frankincense high into the golden dome. Carts and hooves clattered like dry bones after sacrifice. Slaves called dreary song, heaved roped blocks of stone along Via Sacra. Marcia and I stepped from the atrium with a guard, pink amphorae resting on our heads like vulture crowns. Hush draped the market. No one looked at us, not the baker stacking loaves nor the woman arranging baskets of womb red pomegranates. I imagined Mother dressed in a silk stola, handing out oranges to orphans begging on the street. And then I saw him, standing outside the basilica, tall among knights daring each other with debate and wine. Eyes the colour of distant storm darkened mine, catching my left cheek rouged with heat. I carried his gaze to Egeria Spring. We washed our feet with holy water. Water to cleanse sacra, water to cleanse virgin bodies. The guard plunged urns while we sat in shade, chanting hymns of purification, laying wildflowers as offerings. In the still water of the grotto, I saw Mother. How could my eyes be forbidden if I have money enough to buy slaves?

Vivum Sepultus—Buried Alive

Little moth, I hear the hiss
of your wings
singed on dying flame.
It is too dark now
to see your shadow fly
or watch the last drops of oil
sputter in a clay lamp.
Bloody entrails of a still born calf
told of my love for Vetutius.
Our imagined kiss.

Little moth, where was Father
when they gagged and tied me
to the litter and paraded me
through Rome? Why
did my five sisters
spill rumours like wine?
Let them pretend
they have not killed me,
buried me alive
in a wicked field.
Bones will tell the story.
Fear contracts my lungs and
stifles my useless cries for Mother.
Be still now, little moth.
I do not believe in Vesta.
Do you hear shovelled earth
falling like drops of rain?

III. AFTER 39 YEARS, A PHOTOGRAPH SPEAKS

Passport

Torn from a passport, page three rests on a sill near my desk.
Pale green and pinholed with numbers, it filters
sunlight from the garden.

Melbourne has faded. So has the date, 22 *August* 1967.
Rutted letters keyed on a typewriter.
Stamped in purple,

signed by an official with flamboyant loops in his script.
And below, my mother's careful print.
Sharp capitals, a faint hyphen.

Her remarried name, dotted and crossed with a fountain pen.
A passport photo with snipped corners shows
half a family.

Three sisters dressed in cream skivvies, buttoned into
Ladybird cardigans. Their mother, her gaze
more carefree than I remember.

Fine cheekbones, an Elizabeth Taylor beauty—
she wears an argyle knit and dark lipstick.
I sit on her lap, stare into a black lens.

Wisps of hair frame baby brow. Thinking eyes,
downturned mouth. My early panic,
a sudden hiss and snap of light.

Storm Boy

On those warm school days when the bell rang after lunch, our class bounded inside to the cool, grey linoleum corridor. We ran through a hanging garden of school bags, our legs tangling as we pushed ahead to arrive first at the door. Our teacher, a soft-eyed man, waited in silence for us to settle, pair up and hold hands. We all wanted to let go; to escape boy germs and girl germs, especially the warty grasp of Paul Zubov or the hectic arm swinging of Bradley Spargo. Now, quiet as Zen monks, we stole to our desks, slid along wooden seats to our places, folded both hands upon the writing slopes. Mr Genat sat on a slab of table, wearing short shorts, a safari shirt, long socks pulled high from his sandals. He palmed his beard with one hand, leafed each well-thumbed page, searching for today's chapter. Tick tick of a lone fan. Fidgeting whispers flared to a titter. And then, his voice poured into the room, deep and steady as whale song. The world swivelled; his words carried us. Words like *windswept* and *tussocky* netted us into the lagoon life of a boy who combed dunes with his hermit dad. *White spray darted and writhed in the air like snakes of salt*. We made friends with Mr Percival, an orphaned pelican and *the sun glowed on the bare patches of the sandhills and lit up the bushes and tussocks till every stem and twig shone with rosy fire*. Storm Boy knew something about beauty and loss. As our teacher winged his way through the final paragraph, I rested my head upon the desk and listened.

Bully

Ivor Jensen waited for me around a corner, between the tuckshop and my classroom, the sheer bulk of him casting a shadow longer and wider than I imagined, and even though I knew he was trying to show off to my older sister, I trembled when he threatened to lift up his shirt and bare the angry scar stretched across his belly, unless I handed him money, which was the five cents Mum gave me on Fridays to buy two pink musk sticks or an all-day gobstopper, the same size as the golf ball he declared he had swallowed before he was sliced open by a doctor with a polished knife, dripping blood and the terror of this led me to throw my coin at his feet as he whooped and slipped it in his pocket and perhaps I should thank him for preparing me to face Chubs McKinnon, who had nick-named herself, so she could get in first and start the business of taunting me by climbing on top of the Year 9 toilet cubicles while I frantically tried to remove the blood-soaked pad from my knickers before she could announce *she's on the rag* to the world, which makes me think I should thank her also, for steeling me—against the one who can corner and punish, the one who some days wreaks a bloody self-loathing, the one who bites my nail to its quick.

Cherry

My best friend has an older brother with green eyes that flicker in the firelight on a darkened beach, eyes that catch the rising heat in my cheeks, a heat that feels oh-so-welcome to my budding body, unused to gaze, especially from a boy swilling beer like a man, laughing among mates with salt-bleached hair, who wear alpaca jumpers with Peruvian designs, while I wish I wasn't wearing my Snoopy nightshirt beneath a windcheater I pulled on after kissing my parents good night and sneaking out the bedroom window into a wash of midsummer moon, sandy road quiet beneath bare feet, my best friend and I swearing to keep each other's secrets, like the Shush a week later, when her brother led me by the hand from the floral rollaway in her bedroom to his bunk for another kind of sleepover, one where I stare at faded surfing posters that peel from his ceiling, until I'm crouching on a Hot-Buttered tri-fin, nose riding with perfect balance, trailing one hand inside the foam of a barrel, swallowed by a wall of ocean, oblivious to danger, oblivious to the swelling wave he's riding, both of us deafened by the scream of blue water, too loud for me to feel a thing, too loud for him to hear me say *Stop*.

Onion

When I fry onion and push the pearly dice around the pan,
  I think of my mother.

The peeling and chopping are done, it's the beginning
  of something good—shepherd's pie served warm.

Oil and butter loosen and mix in the pan, gilding each piece
  like a pungent star.

Amid the hiss and spit of crushed garlic, I remember
  my mother lifting down

the pressure cooker, always someone to feed—home early,
  home late. I'd watch her pour split peas,

lay down a pink ham hock in boiling stock. I'd wait
  for the noisy rattle to rise and rise

until the cat flattened its ears and the safety valve shrilled.
  Now I hear music when I cook. My mother's music.

Tonight, it's Hoagy Carmichael. Stirring onion, singing Skylark,
  I feel the ache of those songs

and the years we didn't speak. I think of our phone call
  this morning—the usual news, a fresh recipe shared.

I push diced onion around the pan until it softens
  and turns gold.

Guan Yu

There's a statue that sits inside my parents' front door,
next to a ginger jar crowded with canes and umbrellas.

Carved from rosewood he crouches on tangled roots,
as though he has something to say. I see him

through narrow panes as I reach out to knock. Fierce
warrior, phoenix eyed, he bears a dragon blade

and his long beard flows east. I never could tell
if he was smiling. As a child I tried not to look.

Today I see him. Guan Yu. Loyal hero. Saint of war.
The dog barks my arrival and I hear distant halloos

as they make their long walk down the short hallway.
The door opens. Guan Yu sees how far we have come.

The Last Conversation

I have with my father is more business meeting
than farewell. A hot December afternoon,
propped on pillows in bed, he inhales cool air,
blown from a Mistral fan whirring on a table.
He puffs through his final agenda.
A finger jabs the air, speech elusive since the stroke.
My mother, too restless to stay, tired of his pretending
he's still in charge, wheels her frame to the kitchen,
where she clinks plates and glasses into the dishwasher.

Earlier, we visit the doctor, who listens to questions
and his failing heart. He holds my father's hand
and nods when I say I will cancel my holiday.
Don't! my father commands later, at home,
hitting the bedsheet at words that won't come.
Wild-eyed, he gestures as I guess in a game
of charades. My father hates wasting money.
He taught me about risk and the bottom line.
Don't cancel, he says. *What if I don't die?*

Everything Has Been Said

Half an hour before my father dies,
I write to myself. *A strange slumber party,*
I'm wearing old pyjamas for comfort.

The nurse smiles as she folds out
my sofa bed and tucks the sheets
drum tight. *How will I know?*

She holds my question like a kind parent,
checks his chart and leaves. I search
my laptop for answers—*purpling skin, cool hands.*

I look at him. He lies in bed, propped
to one side like a listing vessel, facing me
with his eyes closed, thinned lashes glistening.

Smooth olive brow, quiet breath pulsing
the loose skin at his throat. His mouth
just open, as if he could say something.

I hold his warm hand. The deepening blue
of his nails, a clue. And I write again.
I am not frightened. Nothing can be altered.

The Urn

My mother sits with her back to a locked cabinet of display urns. Teardrops, hearts and silver birds rest on glass shelves. We are talking options with Dianne. She slides a Simply Beautiful brochure across the desk. A vase embossed with butterflies and blossom, *is our most popular urn*, a hand-crafted box in maple or oak, engraved with a seascape. Mum is perched on the edge of a beige tub chair. Her hands grip the brakes of her walker. She looks past an ocean sunset painted onto a scattering-tube. There are other designs too—ascending doves, a field of forget-me-nots and a starry night. *Take your time*. Dianne straightens her black skirt and leaves to collect paperwork and my father's remains. Bronze plaques stud a memorial lawn outside the window, unfurling toward the Garden of Serenity. Blousy pink roses bow their heads in the rain. She returns with a blue box, the kind you might purchase shoes in. Mum stifles a noise, a soft stridor breath as my father is placed on the desk. She doesn't choose an urn or a vase or a tube. I tap a PIN into a cash machine and pick up the box. Mum wheels herself to the front entrance. We head out under a shared umbrella, and I am startled by how much a father weighs.

After 39 Years, a Photograph Speaks

Look at this: a family of twelve, blended
and extended, gathers around a lounge
that blooms cabbage roses.

They pose after dinner in the sitting room.
Adults except for a spectacled nephew,
cross-legged on the floor.

Your aunt and uncle visiting from California.
He's behind the camera showing you
how to smile with your teeth.

Say Hersh—eys! You're squeezed together, seated
with your three sisters and a moustached
brother-in-law. He's a psychiatrist,

handy during those later years. Two more brothers-in-law
stand behind with your parents and aunt.
One, a young Al Pacino, the other, Jesus.

Your father in yet another illustrated shirt.
Open necked, with brown etchings
—gondolas moored on the Grand Canal.

He clasps your mother so she is angled toward him.
Her geometric dress, her wedding pearls.
She doesn't look at the camera.

Instead, she smiles at you. Your aunt, soft waves
of American hair, stands next to her brother
in his gondola shirt. She doesn't know

she'll be alive at 101, her mind as clear as a diamond.
There is so much that's unknown. One sister
will die young. No Jesus can save her.

Tilt me like a hologram and you'll sense something
leaks. A father's noxious secret seeps
through the family. Invisible as hydrogen,

until a sister lights the match.

IV. ULYSSES

Coming Home

Sometime between yesterday and tomorrow,
I wake to the moon, bright on the plane's wing.
My right cheek judders, as night speeds past the window,
spinning air like sugar. I've been sleeping, dreaming
New Mexico sky. Bold, lapis brushstrokes shot with cloud,
ranging high above Sangre de Cristo.
A snow-capped Sierra rising from grassland,
slopes stippled with pinyon and juniper.

I doze, replaying the gardens of Upaya.
Bleached trunks and new lime growth
on birch trees, silver sage, burnt yellow mounds
of rabbit brush, pale, bowing blooms on the yuccas.
Each morning, I sat at the kitchen table enfolded
in pink adobe walls, drinking green tea,
writing and watching red capped house finches
gather at the feeder outside.

I wake again. The plane dips beneath
cloud to early morning. Sydney is dark, slick
with rain and glimmering headlights, as cars trail
their way to work. I think of that last day, looking
out to see the sky change to gauze. The unexpected
snowfall in spring dusting the cottonwoods and lilacs.
A frosted statue of Buddha beneath a flowering
dogwood, eyes gazing down at the red earth.

Postcard

—for Charlie

An apricot sky fades to gold then blue outside our window.
    Two palms in green skirts touch fronds and the ocean drifts sideways
        with a calm break that I can't see below the windowsill.

I hear the kettle and your phone click as you scroll the feed.
    You worry, make plans, search for answers hidden in a tiny screen.
        You bring me tea and ask if I'd like to swim. I say nothing.

You say it's not a trick question. My tongue is unplugged, my mind
    softer than a baby bird. You lie next to me and fold my hand
        in yours. You smoothe your thumb over each of my fingernails.

We are perfectly still. I want to stay in this postcard,
    send it to myself. I'll pin it above my desk, show it
        to our children. I'll send it to your new phone. Click.

            I wish we were here.

Ocean Pool

We come to the pool feeling flat as leaking lilos,
our ears full of squabble and demands for ice cream.

We've left them behind on the sand to work out who
will bury who and how to live without parents

for an hour while we remember how to be together,
even though you don't like to swim. I snap on a cap,

tighten my goggles and slip into the cool. You sit
on the edge staring over a beach dotted with castles

and children surfing or picking their way across
stone platforms until they reach Jump Rock.

Beyond lies the headland, recovering from fire,
its charred tree line a whiskered stubble

growing on, in spite of it all. *Go on then*, you say,
looking down at me. Bubbles cascade from my nose.

Some catch and sit along my fingers like tiny pearls
until I swing my first stroke, take a breath

from my arm's blue arc. Through scratched goggles
I watch the sunlight move on the sandy pool floor,

a luminous filigree that steadies me until I am swimming
my own rhythm, an upbeat relief. And I forget you,

until your flippered feet explode past, stirring up
the sand and water into a furious, foaming wake.

I stop swimming and drift to the end, where you wait,
ruddy and breathless as a new lover.

Cowlick

—for Will

Tucked in a tussle of fireweed and kikuyu, he could be mistaken for a boulder or charred log, except for the quiver of dew lacing the tips of his ears. Cutting the engine, I watch his breath mist from glistening nostrils into mauve light. The dog noses my jacket for warmth. We watch the calf raise his clumsy head from folded forelegs. Black pearls veiled beneath an awning of eyelashes. Velvet ears cup the air, listening for his mother, as she walks a steady rhythm back to him. For the first time, I understand the word—*cowlick*. The dark whorl of fur, styled into an abundant toupee by his mother's black tongue before she hid him in the grass.

I longed to keep you safe, tried to hide your swirling mischief, buttoned you into clean shirts, pulled up your long grey socks. Wiping milk from your boy mouth didn't stop your stream of questions, nor your classroom wheel of chaos, all the red pen teacher notes. Please forgive my instincts. It was a doctor who told me it was time to pull away. To let you graze among the apple gums and run freely on strong legs.

January Water Dragons

All summer he watches me heft my basket
down the grassy slope and slip on fallen longan fruit.

Today, he lies on sandstone, next to the pegs,
pressing a push up, with muscled forearms, a rusted belly.

He wears reptilian plaid. A grey, nubbled suit
splashed with ink. A tiny crest runs down his spine,

and he's still, except for one sweeping eye.
A small, dark moon ringed with gold. Peg by peg,

towel by towel, sheets and shorts, I move along
the clothesline. My bare legs. His black claws.

I taste salt on my top lip. Two towels away from him
I drop a peg. His head begins to bob and tilt, a warning

to his hidden harem. A dragoness tail disappears in a thin
streak through the fence. Others run like overwound toys

through a flurry of leaves up a loquat tree. I collect
my basket, he lies still again, eye half closed. At the back door,

three baby dragons drink from a dripping tap. We are tenants
in their kingdom, living on summer's lease. I step closer,

the babies slide into the drain. They swim as water eddies
and pulls them into a pipe, back to the garden and beyond.

Tonight, the Lion is Here

Right here, near our jeep. An open jeep
without a roof, windows or doors.
In the moonlight, he patrols thickets,

yellow finger grass that borders
his pride land. I slide down the seat
and watch with one eye.

My sons whisper in the front seat
as Patrick changes the spotlight lens
to a rosy glow.

The lion shakes his mane, raises his vast
forehead from the earth to inhale night.
Amber eyes close and his mouth pulls

apart in a curling grimace. Four scimitar teeth
catch light as he tastes air, lifts his black
thatched tail and grunts.

Giant testes bob like fruit. He sprays bursts
of urine into scrub. For days,
we have searched for him.

Along riverbeds at dusk where Egyptian geese
rise in pairs from reeds and fly low
over dark water,

where Goliath herons step their faith
around crocodiles, mouths half open
in the fading heat

and slick hippopotamus leave the river
with bellies as pink as newborns
to graze all night.

We comb Mopane woodlands among rust
and golden branches and the deepest shadows
of a Winterthorn forest.

Tonight the lion is here, padding toward the jeep,
toward my seat. And just when I want to call
out like a startled puku,

a breeze seduces him with a new scent.
He turns, walks away—
a shiver in the grass.

Ulysses Butterfly

—for Tish

I don't remember how we began—
two pearls glued to a misted leaf,
among ribbonwood and fern,
away from quick tongued geckos,
the prying antennae of katydids.

Our blue-winged mothers
chose a Euodia tree, a tender nursery
for fat caterpillars. Solemn call
of emerald doves *tiwooing* secrets
through our waxen shells.

Other butterflies flickered
shadows outside our eggs,
sipped ginger flowers in the heat.
A kaleidoscope of jezebels,
wingspans wide as the sun.

The rupture—our green and yellow
grub bodies. Spikes dressed our backs,
spoke poison to the shrike thrush.
Mandibles munching leaf.
Our hunger. O the hunger!

Do you remember the silence of silk?
The quiet cool of chrysalis.
After spinning, hanging upside down
like small green fruit. Time ceased
and we dreamed of wings.

You flew first. Frantic gem.
Rapid darting blue,
long black tails lifting high
into the canopy of a Kauri.
Light spilled from basket ferns.

I don't remember days passing,
our closing wings at dusk,
huddled on a bough of satin ash.
Nor the glow of ghost fungi,
slow moss mending earth.

You, I will remember—
looping grace through tangled vines,
drawn by pink bursts on branches.
We rest on candied tendrils,
taste flowers with our feet.

A Life of Birds

—for my father-in-law, David

Somewhere in Russia, a great grey owl
rests in a larch tree listening for lemmings
burrowing beneath snow. Her head swivels
like a radar, sweeping the quiet for sound.

In South Africa, a lanner falcon turns in the sky,
scanning the plains for sparrows.
Black onyx eyes narrow as she plucks prey
from flight. You, lover of birds, watch them

glide on TV and forget you're here,
lying upon a new bedspread, patterned
with forest and fern. White hair, soft
and washed. Thin legs lost in beige trousers.

Still, except for short, quick rises of your chest.
We marvel at bee hummingbirds in the woodlands
of Cuba. Tiny, iridescent connoisseurs sip nectar
from red flowers with rapid wings and hearts.

Later, you tell me apostle birds crowd your back step
in grey suits waiting for grain, like bookies in the ring,
while you pull on boots and plait a new thong for your whip.
Magpies patrol your silver beet in glossy tuxedoes

pulling grubs after rain. Blue wrens (those cornflower bandits)
hop and chit among the poplars that line your driveway
and willy wagtails hitch jaunty rides on the backs of sheep.
In the furthest paddock, wedge-tailed eagles high in red gums

watch you mend fences. They soar without wing beat
in the thermal currents of noon. But it's the teal ducks
you admire from your blue ute. How they rise
from the channel at dusk like a perfect chord.

Sisterhood

—Blanco museum, Ubud

Nancy poses for photos in the museum garden—
a wreathed hornbill surprise for visitors who step

through the stone portico to walk a path greened with fern.
Outside the birdhouse, she perches on the lowest branch

of a flamboyant tree, with a yellow macaw named Brian.
Her beak curves like a pair of bony secateurs, tooth-edged,

stained orange from papaya. She holds it open, switch-sidles
her black heft on squat legs along the roost onto my bare arm.

Cool tripod feet press lightly into skin. Perhaps it's her long
lashes that blink down the sun, the vermilion skin that rings

her buttoned eyes or the turquoise pouch that adorns her throat.
Or maybe it's her Mohican crest expertly styled by breeze

that has earned her name. In the wild, she raises her clutch
in a tree crevice walled in by fruit pulp and dung. She soars

above the forest canopy with a wing beat whooshing louder
than a steam engine. Worshipped as an omen bird, a messenger

from the gods, Nancy fixes me with an Eocene stare and
plucks the bruised frangipani bloom from behind my ear.

Rembulan Spa
—Ubud

Soon, Sutri will paint my nails magenta,
        the colour of dragonfruit, while I rest
    in the deep curve of a teak chair.

She takes my left hand and kneads it
        with long fingers stretching
    my palm until I am an Apsara,

loose enough to float my celestial limb
        in a bowl of sandalwood water. She holds
    my right hand and studies the thumb,

tsking at the torn, reddened cuticle
        bitten by disquiet, misshapen over years.
    I want to close my hand like a lotus bud.

Instead, I watch her dab pale pink cream,
        until the skin cools. Sutri props my thumb
    with hers, paints with steady strokes.

She fans dry these mended hands
        And I think of my sister, washing my hair
    when I was a child. Her careful combing

and quiet talk. Warm water falling
        through smooth strands.
    I taste the sweetness of fruit.

Glamour Nails

We sit side by side, on vinyl recliners, a newly crowned king and queen. Our backs are kneaded and pummelled like bread dough. Your deep voice judders above the froth and bubble of footbaths. I was curious when you asked to join me for a mani-pedi at Glamour Nails. Now, I listen to you talk after three years of teen grunts. *Yeah. Nuh. Stuff.* Lin runs more hot water into our tubs and pours in a steady stream of blue crystals. *You're a lucky Mum. Such a strong, handsome boy.* You pay little attention to her as you fan the sample nail designs on your lap. I worry that you'll get in trouble at school. *Just one thumb Mum, it'll be fine.* You choose French Bulldog and I choose Kiss me I'm Kind, the latest pale pink in gel. I close my eyes and we're quiet for a while.

Last week you took a girl to a formal. You were excited for weeks about the beauty of corsage blooms and your new Italian suit. That evening, you called and asked me to pick you up early. Silence filled the car as we drove home around the bay. On the salon wall hangs a picture of two perfect hands with nails like painted moons, clasping an Arum lily. A young woman finishes the ears of your bulldog with a fine brush while Lin trims my cuticles. And then you tell me something I have always known.

Quiet Zone
—for Samuel

There are many kinds of happiness.
You sit opposite me at a table for two

in the Mitchell Library, next to the Dixson
card catalogue. Your horn-rimmed glasses

match the neat, teak drawers with yellowed labels.
I watch you scratch words with your favourite pen—

blue, the cap lightly chewed. You'll lay it
down, open a laptop and press in new earbuds.

Slender fingers type, sometimes stopping
to finger-comb your hair. You're listening

to a countertenor sing *Ombra fedela anch'io*.
Above us, light pours through a glass ceiling

and runs down three tiers of blackwood.
A curling bronze staircase leads

to old volumes of red, navy and brown.
Griffins, urns and rosettes crowd

a travertine frieze. Stained glass windows
tell the Canterbury tales. A long hand

on the old clock bounces with each minute.
The air is warm, muggy with books.

At fourteen, there are days when you
don't speak beyond one syllable.

Here, we're not allowed to talk.
For once, it doesn't matter.

A Portrait of My Mother as a Butterfly

All morning, a flutter of monarchs
pilot the puffballs of milkweed. Each slips
inside tiny mauve bells, dusting its feet with gold.

When the nurse says she's fond of my mother,
I want to cry. Mum calls the nurse by name,
asks about her family. She's popular among residents.

One follows me as I walk the stone path.
Tiger-bright wings cup and catch the air, flicker past
my ankles. It dips ahead in thin sunlight, over and over.

My mother was once a nurse. She cared for frail people
in ageing cottages. Some school holidays, I would come
and watch as she opened windows to let in fresh air.

They're known for endurance. A slow wing beat carries
them thousands of miles each migration. It takes generations
to find home, even with a soul in their antennae.

The first person I met who was ninety was Mrs Fraser. She sat all day
in a recliner padded with sheepskin, mottled legs resting on a stool.
Mum chatted as she held her wrist, a silver watch counting the pulse.

Instead of sleeping, monarchs cluster in trees at dusk.
With wings closed, they become dried leaves, shivering
to keep warm and protected. Sometimes branches break.

Hands like paperbark, Albert lost his sight at Gallipoli.
Milky eyes roamed above my head as we talked football
and Mum changed sheets. She brought him home for a roast.

Monarchs drink from flowers or sip moisture from puddles
after a nice rain. When they aren't nectaring or puddling,
they roll their proboscis up like a pillow under their head.

My father was handsome, charming, in fact, so Mum refused
his proposal three times before yielding. She was happiest
at work, flitting from house to house, tending to her patients.

Imagine beauty as poison. Monarchs feed on milkweed. Toxic sap
sours their larvae, protects them from predators. If eaten by humans,
nerves cease to fire. Eat enough and hearts will stop.

On Sundays, my father would sit Mum down to reconcile
cheque stubs from her handbag with their bank book,
the room paralysed by his tut-tutting and her explanations.

Some people say, if a monarch flies away from you
it's a sign to let go — old grief, estrangements, lost time.
The monarch knows life is brief. Death is not to be feared.

Mum calls. She's been asked to buddy a new resident this week.
I picture them together, landing in the dining room with a view
of English trees and leaves that colour and fall with the seasons.

Barrenjoey

That time of year has come when pines draw
    long shadows on the sand of late afternoon.

    Smooth and cool as terracotta beneath my feet.
I walk the curved spit to reach the headland,

as I do each day to quieten thoughts that run
    too fast, that dart like minnows. Looking up,

    I see slabs of stone, sombre as Lewis Chessmen.
A sea eagle glides on titanic wings.

A squall offshore whips chaos and stirs white caps.
    But here at the tide's edge, water spills

    and sweeps neat lines of foam into a crosshatched shore,
where a rogue wave rushes my ankles, startling

me with its strength. I stand and wait for the ebb
    to soften the surge and rinse my bare feet clean.

Origin

I begin in the slow press of my father's foot
upon a pedal, as he glides his dull green Holden
to the bottom of Curzon Hill.

Beside a picket fence garlanded with hedges
of mock orange, he spies you, a slender widow
in black capri pants and ballet flats.

An Audrey Hepburn mirage — O those cheekbones —
the small hands of your daughters hold yours,
as you wait for a lift.

How many times did he squeeze the brakes
before inviting you to dinner? What if
he'd turned the corner at Brett Street?

What if he hadn't served you tinned soup and a chicken
from Mr Pickles the grocer, if he hadn't taken you
to the Great Northern for Chateaubriand,

if he hadn't introduced you to his motherless daughters
(how your heart ached for them), if he hadn't
asked you to marry him three times,

if he hadn't booked the cathedral before he proposed,
if you hadn't caved in (your words, not mine),
if he wasn't so *goddamned charming*?

You wouldn't have worn that beaded dress, a chiffon turban
that caught drifts of confetti. You would never, ever,
have agreed to another baby.

This morning when the nurse left your room, you told me
you wish you had left him. I brushed your white hair,
grateful you didn't.

BIOGRAPHY

ALISON GORMAN is a poet, teacher, and former speech pathologist who lives in Sydney. Her poetry has appeared in *Cordite*, *Island*, *Honest Ulsterman*, *Meanjin*, *Mslexia*, *Popshot Quarterly*, *Southerly* and *Southword*. She was awarded the Dorothy Porter Poetry Prize in 2016 and a Varuna Residential Fellowship in 2023. Her poems have been shortlisted in the 2024 Gwen Harwood Poetry Prize, the Bridport Poetry Prize, the Fish Poetry Prize and the Mslexia Poetry Competition. Her pamphlet was highly commended in the 2024 Mslexia Pamphlet Competition, shortlisted in the Cinnamon Press Literature Awards the same year, and was a finalist in the Fool for Poetry International Chapbook Competition in 2022. She has an MA in Creative Writing from the University of Sydney. When Alison is not writing poetry, she teaches creative writing to children at Inkling Writing Studio, which she founded in 2018.

NOTES

"*Telling Will*" was prompted by a poem by Sharon Olds, "Telling My Mother," from *Stag's Leap* (Knopf, 2012).

"*About Secrets*" was prompted by the opening line of Mila Haugová's poem, "To My Daughter About Love."

"*A Woman Talks to Her Tongue*" was prompted by the title of a poem by Anna Swir, "A Woman Talks to Her Thigh."

"*Eulogy on the Flapper*" is the title of an article written by Zelda Fitzgerald and published by *Metropolitan Magazine* in June, 1922.

"*Viva La Vida*" was inspired by the painting of the same name by Frida Kahlo, 1954.

"*Venus and Mars*" was inspired by the painting of the same name by Sandro Botticelli, c. 1485.

"*Ghost Ranch*, 1949" was inspired by the painting "Ram's head with Hollyhock," by Georgia O'Keeffe, 1935.

"*Princess of Silence*" was inspired by Enheduanna, the earliest known poet whose name has been recorded. Words from her hymns appear in italics.

"*The House of Vesta*" imagines the experience of Aemilia, a vestal virgin, who was condemned to death in 114BC for violating her vow of chastity.

"*Storm Boy*" is a classic Australian children's novel written by Colin Thiele (Rigby, 1964).

"*The Last Conversation*," "*Everything has been said*" and "*The Urn*" were prompted by themes in *The Father*, by Sharon Olds (Cape, 2009).

"*Ulysses Butterfly*" was inspired by a tapestry created by my mother-in-law Tish and prompted by a poem by Maya Chowdhry, "*Butterfly Orchid*."

5 islands PRESS

BRIGHT CROCKERY DAYS: THE POETRY OF ROBERT GRAY

Essays

Mark Tredinnick (ed)

August 2024

In *Bright Crockery Days*, eminent writers and artists choose their favourite poem by Gray and speak about how it works and how it touches them, what it has meant to them, and why it matters so much to all of us. The book is an anthology, then, of much of Robert Gray's best work, chosen by some who have known him; and it is a collection of trim essays that read those poems closely, elucidating and celebrating some of the poet's best-known and most-loved pieces.

Although each essay examines an individual poem, contributors range freely across Gray's work, placing it in the context of their own lives, and of the poet's life and work, and speaking of the place each poem occupies in Australian culture, in contemporary literature, and in the poetic tradition at large. The result is Robert Gray in three dimensions—a manifold, astute and affectionate reading of a great poet's life and work through poems from those who know and love him best.

Bright Crockery Days is edited by Mark Tredinnick; contributors include Judith Beveridge, Robbie Coburn, John Foulcher, Luke Fischer, Kevin Hart, Sarah Holland-Batt, Geoffrey Lehmann, Judith Nangala Crispin, Geoff Page, Brigitte Ross, Lindsay Tuggle, and Todd Turner.

5 Islands PRESS

THE MAKING OF A POEM:
ELEVEN AUSTRALIAN POETS TALK ABOUT THEIR CRAFT

Rosanna McGlone

January 2025

The Making of a Poem is an exploration of the craft of poetry. It provides a rare insight into how poems are made, exploring a poem's journey from a rough draft into its final form. The book showcases a wide variety of forms and redrafting techniques from free verse to prose poetry, from sonnet to Abecedarian.

ROSANNA McGLONE's book examines the poetic practice of a cross-section of Australia's most accomplished and celebrated poets. The poets come from across Australia, from Western Australia to Queensland, and differ widely in age and ages and backgrounds. But the contributors are united in their outstanding level of achievement and in their willingness to share their redrafting process. The book explores the development of a single poem by each poet, capturing its unique the unique way in which each poem has been developed, and exploring questions such as the place of personal experience in poetry and how content is married with form.

Editor Rosanna McGlone is a writer and journalist whose features have appeared in numerous outlets including *The Weekend Australian*, *The Sydney Morning Herald*, *The Age*, *The Guardian* and *Salon.com*. Her earlier book featuring UK poets, *The Process of Poetry*, was number one on Amazon in the UK, featured on BBC Radio 4's Front Row and has been widely taught in British universities.

Contributing poets are Judith Beveridge, Gavin Yuan Gao, Sarah Holland-Batt, John Kinsella, Anthony Lawrence, Bella Li, Audrey Molloy, Judith Nangala Crispin, Sarah M Saleh, Jaya Savige, and Mark Tredinnick.

5 Islands PRESS

THE ZEBRA PATH OF TREE LIGHT

Kai Jensen

April 2025

The Zebra Path of Tree Light is a linguistic and emotional adventure, which you're invited to join. The poems express Jensen's love of art and literature and are coloured in bright and dark tones by his travels, by Buddhism, by a loving marriage to a psychotherapist who is also a fabric artist, and by a sober view of life's challenges and disappointments.

Kai Jensen's poetry ranges from personal narrative and captured scenes, through the playful and the speculative, to postmodern forms such as erasure poems. The broad range of his intellect and experience is evident in this collection; the book is full of delightful surprises: stripping the bed linen to a retreat in a Thai monastery; the difficulty of making a quilt look its best for a photograph; a sojourn on an asteroid; reflections on the game of chess; redactions of the letters of Virgina Woolf.

In these gentle and reflective poems, Jensen examines everyday anxieties, including the process of ageing, maintaining a delicate balance between empathy and irony. Combining skilful, sometimes exuberant, wordplay with careful observation, they manifest a maturity and wisdom based on long contemplation of life and letters.

KAI JENSEN lives, works and writes on Yuin Country, at Wallaga Lake on the New South Wales Far South Coast. Kai was born in Philadelphia in 1959; from the age of five, he lived in Aotearoa/ New Zealand, and he moved to Australia in 2004, where he is now an Australian citizen. Kai's poetry was interrupted by his career as a university manager, but since moving to Wallaga Lake in 2017 he has resumed writing poetry and sending it out for publication, while continuing to work as an editor and a consultant to universities.